Hi, I'm *Lauren* And I Have *Autism* But– I Have *Jesus* Too

Lauren Breaux with Barb and Matt Breaux

ISBN 979-8-88851-760-4 (Paperback)
ISBN 979-8-88851-762-8 (Hardcover)
ISBN 979-8-88851-761-1 (Digital)

Covenant Books
11661 Hwy 707
Murrells Inlet, SC 29576
www.covenantbooks.com

My name is Lauren.

I am *autistic*.

BUT-

God made me
and he doesn't make mistakes.

I was created
in his image.

For we are his workmanship—his own master work,
a work of art—created in Christ Jesus.
—Ephesians 2:10 AB

So God created human beings in his image.
Then God looked over all he had made, and it was excellent in
every way.
—Genesis 1:27, 31 ICB/TLB

Sometimes I can be so

deep in my
thoughts

in **"my own world,"**

that I don't even hear

when someone is talking

to me.

BUT-

This *super focus* helps me concentrate better when I'm reading or writing. I'm glad I don't get distracted easily.

And I know God is happy when my thoughts stay focused on reading and writing *good things*.

Fix your thoughts on what is true and good and right.

Think about things that are pure and lovely, and
dwell on the fine, good things in others.

Think about all you can praise God for and be glad about.
—Philippians 4:8 TLB

Sometimes I
don't like the
monotone sound
of my voice.

It makes me
think of a
robot.

But-

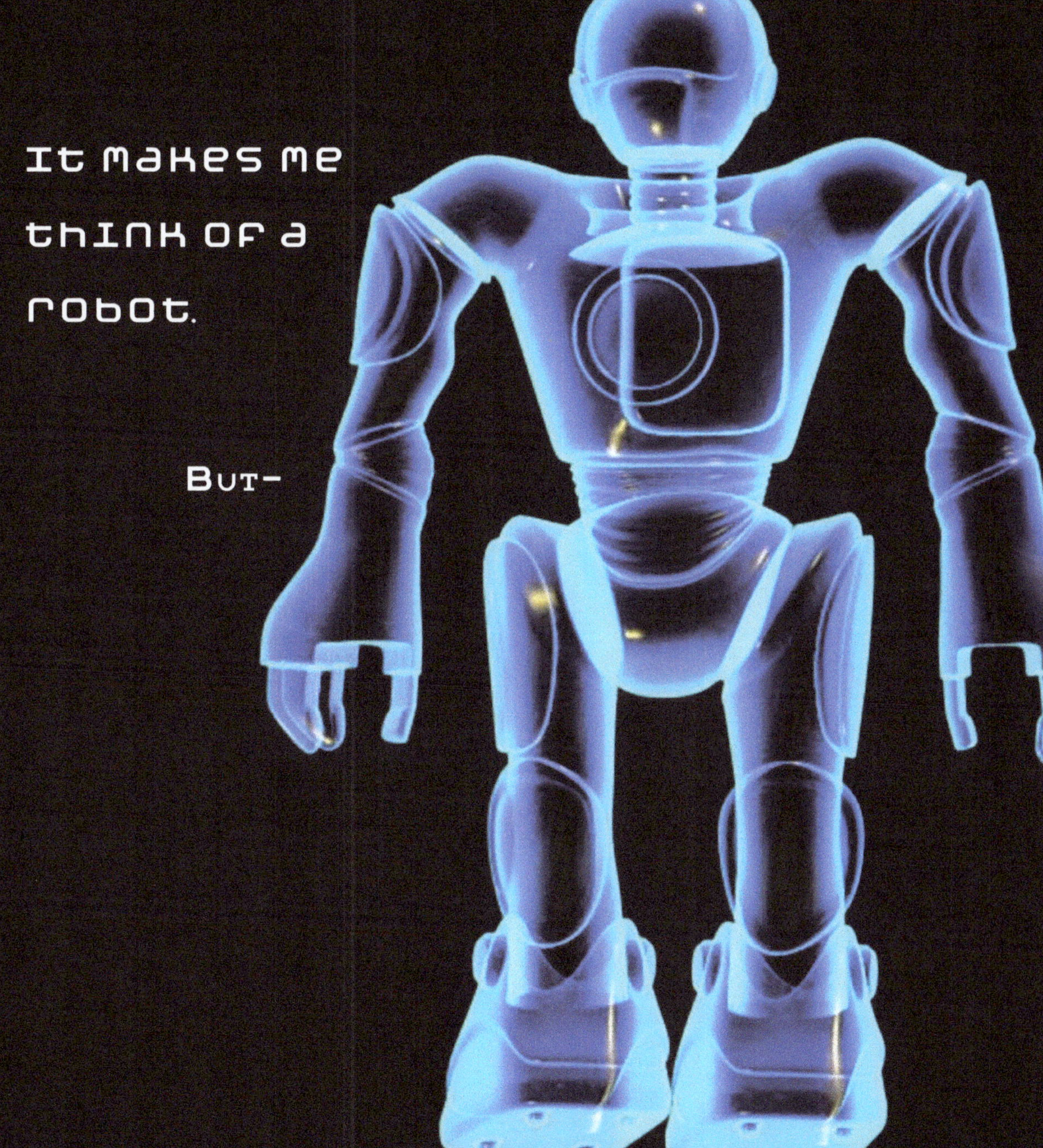

I heard my voice in a family video and
it actually does go
up
and
down when I talk.

God really did know what he was doing
when he made me!

You made my whole being. I praise you because you made me
in an amazing and wonderful way. I know this very well.

You saw my bones being formed as I took shape in my mother's body.

All the days planned for me were written in
your book before I was one day old.
—Psalm 139:13–14, 16 ICB

When I was really young,
I flapped my hand and arm high in the air
and made grunting sounds.

12

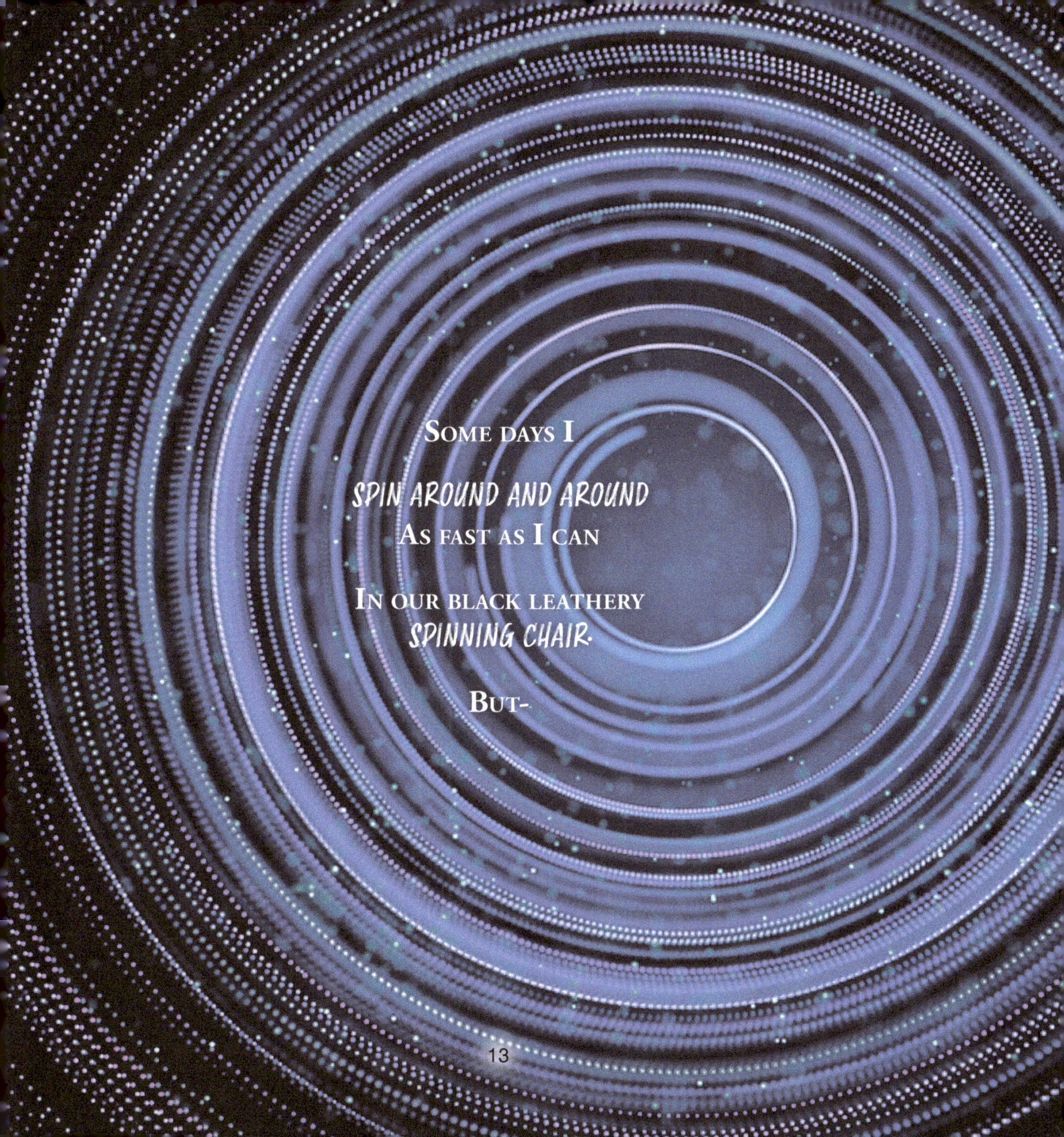

Some days I

Spin around and around
As fast as I can

In our black leathery
Spinning chair.

But-

This is called stimming
and it's okay.

Moving my fingers helps keep
me relaxed and focused.

Spinning around and around
is calming and makes me
feel less anxious.

Don't worry about anything; instead, pray about everything.
Tell God your needs, and don't forget to
thank him for his answers.

If you do this, you will experience God's peace,
which is far more wonderful than the human mind can understand.
—Philippians 4:6–7 TLB

I have to keep the closet door

closed

at night because the
**DARKNESS IS
SCARY.**

I can't go on escalators.

I still get worried and afraid
even after years of trying.

BUT-

I know Jesus is always with me.
Even in the dark.

I don't have to be afraid.
I just have to remember to
give all my fears to him.

Oh, and thank you, Jesus, for *elevators*!

Be strong and courageous. Do not be afraid or terrified.

The Lord your God goes with you; he will
never leave you nor forsake you.
—Deuteronomy 31:6 NIV

I am with you and will watch over you wherever you go.
—Genesis 28:15 NIV

I really like Disney
live-action movies.
I like them so much that I talk
about them and write about
them all the time.

Over and over and over.

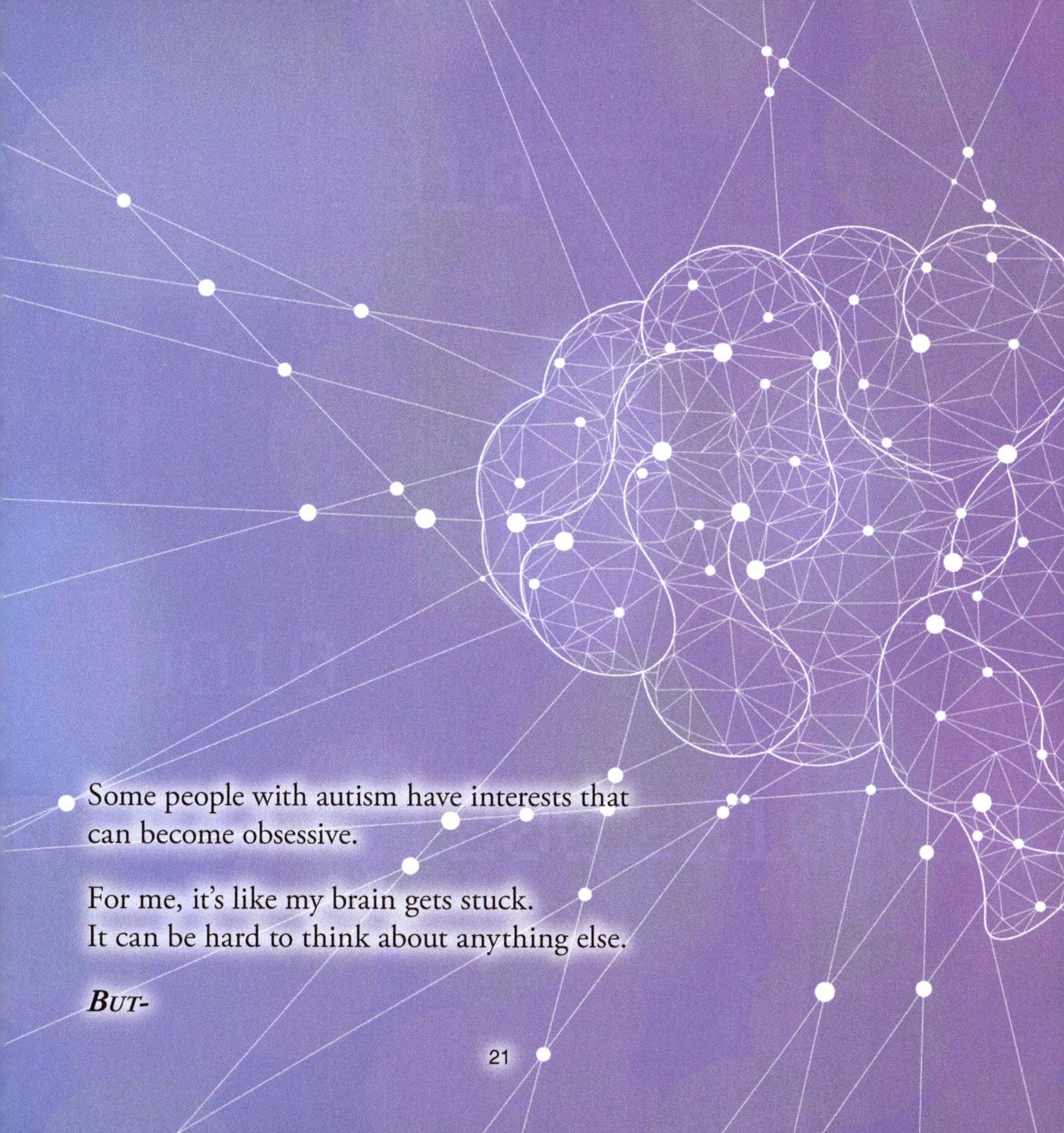

Some people with autism have interests that
can become obsessive.

For me, it's like my brain gets stuck.
It can be hard to think about anything else.

BUT-

I <u>Do</u> have lots of interests to share. I'm blessed to
have caring people in my life who get me.
I'm glad I have a best friend too.
I might repeat the same ideas over and over, but they are happy to listen.

Jesus is another friend who is always with me
and loves to hear what I have to say.

O Lord, you have examined my heart and know
everything about me. You know when I sit or stand.

You know my every thought. Every moment you know where
I am. You know what I am going to say before I even say it.
—Psalm 139:1–4 TLB

I tell my mom and dad that
I'm worried about my tall height.

I also don't like the
way my bottom lip feels.

It's big and rubs against
my teeth.

I'm anxious about growing up too.

My mom joked she could wear
high heels all the time so I feel shorter,
but I know that won't work.

Thanks anyway, Mom.

BUT-

I guess there are some things about
myself that I can't change. That's okay.
God made me special, and he loves me so much.

My brother Tony prays for me every day.
I'm happy when my cat Kiddo licks my face.

AND Dad and I watch cartoons together.
That keeps us both young!

Let him have all your worries and cares, for
he is always thinking about you
and watching everything that concerns you.
—1 Peter 5:7 TLB

Will all your worries add a single moment to your life?

Don't be anxious about tomorrow. God
will take care of your tomorrow.

Live one day at a time.
—Matthew 6:27, 34 TLB

I get very sad and will cry
sometimes when something fun ends.

When my friend went back home
after my birthday party,

I cried myself to sleep.

I've even sobbed in the
middle of an exciting concert
because I was thinking about how I would feel
when it was over.
BUT-

Mom told me
"Don't cry because it's over. Be
happy because it happened."

Mom and Dad say I should focus
on the positive and be grateful.

I will give thanks to you, Lord, with all my heart;
I will tell of all your wonderful deeds.
—Psalm 9:1 NIV

So be truly glad! There is wonderful joy ahead.
—1 Peter 1:6 TLB

I used to like to move the spit
around in my mouth and
make bubbles inside my cheeks.

I liked the way it felt when
the bubbles popped.

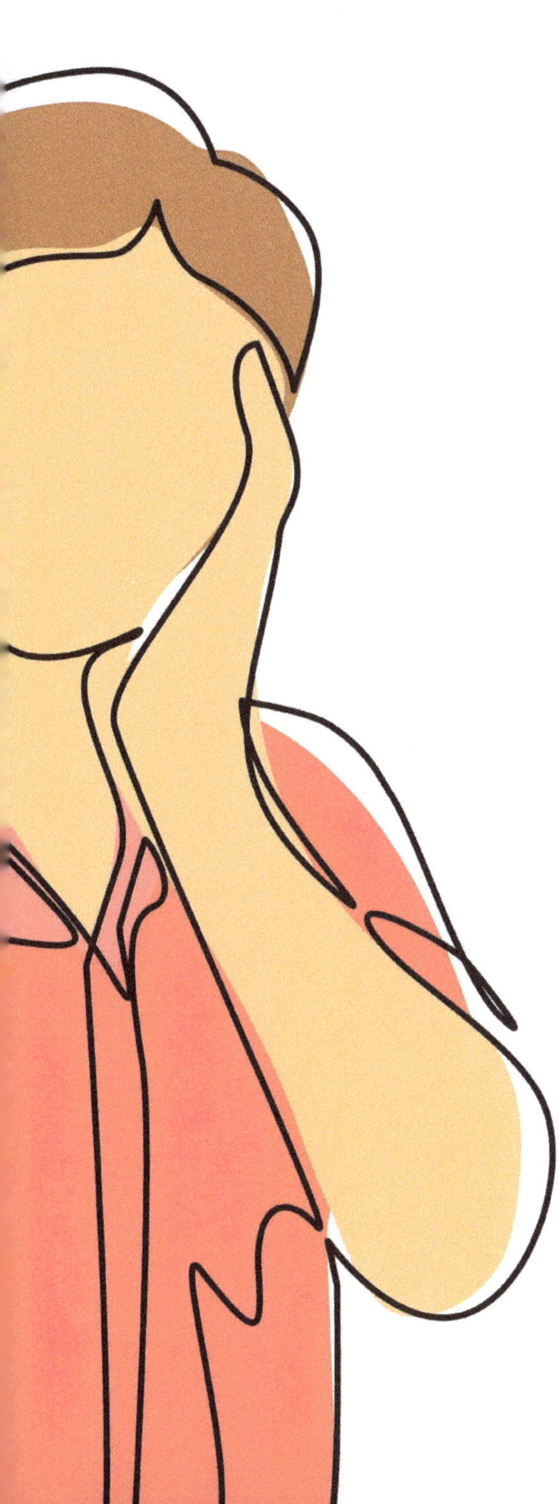

Now I don't like doing it
because my cheeks hurt a lot.

I guess it's become a habit.

BUT-

My occupational
therapist gave me
oral-motor mouth
exercises to do.

I know I can keep
my mouth busy
chewing sugar-free gum too.

I also know that I
can trust Jesus to
give me strength to say
no to bad habits.

So give yourselves humbly to God.
Resist the devil and he will flee from you.
—James 4:7 TLB

I want to remind you that your strength
must come from the Lord's mighty
power within you.

Put on all of God's armor so that you will be able to stand
safe against all strategies and tricks of Satan.
—Ephesians 6:10–11 TLB

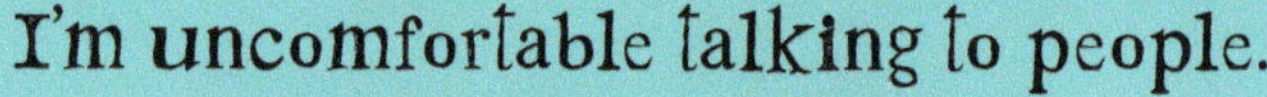

I'm uncomfortable talking to people.

I struggle with
understanding facial
expressions if someone
isn't saying words.

IT'S HARD TO LOOK RIGHT AT
PEOPLE'S FACES AND
KNOW WHAT TO SAY.

SOMETIMES I JUST REPEAT WORDS AND PHRASES

I HEAR FROM TV SHOWS.

BUT-

Most of the time those repeated lines
called echolalia
fit perfectly into the conversation.

Sometimes it can be funny too.
My family loves my quick wit.
They also pray that social situations become easier for me.

How we laughed and sang for joy.
What amazing things the Lord has done.
—Psalm 126:2 TLB

Pray for me, too, and ask God to give me the right
words as I boldly tell others about the Lord.
—Ephesians 6:19 TLB

I don't know how to count money, tell time,

or do simple math problems.

I don't know my left from my right, and

sometimes I put my Velcro shoes on the wrong

feet.

I even put my shirts on

backward sometimes.

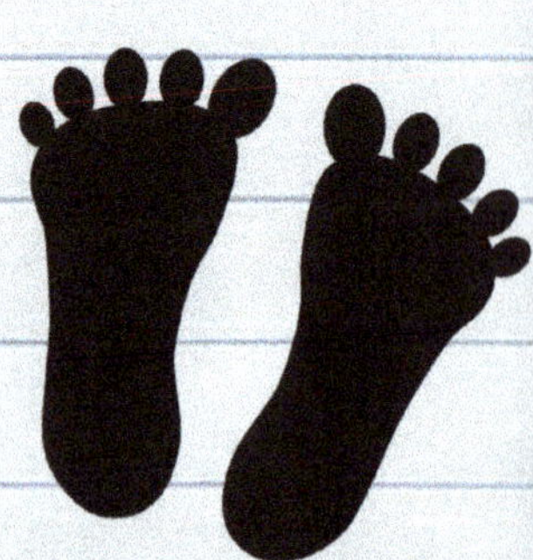

My mom gives me a shower
every morning and lays my
clothes out for the day.
Mom and Dad help me brush
my hair and my teeth.

I can't drive a car
or stay home all by myself.

BUT—

My mom and dad never stop
encouraging me every day.

Most of all, they love and care for me
just the way I am.

What really matters is that I know Jesus.
He loves me, and I love him.
I asked him into my heart, and someday I will be in heaven with him.

Until then, even though I struggle sometimes,
I know God is still working on me.

Thank you, Jesus.

In this world you will have trouble. But take heart!
I have overcome the world.
—John 16:33 NIV

And we know that all that happens to us is working for our
good if we love God and are fitting into his plans.
—Romans 8:28 TLB

For I know the plans I have for you, says the Lord.
They are plans for good and not for evil,
to give you a future and a hope.

—Jeremiah 29:11 TLB

Do you want to know Jesus like I do?

The Bible says that God created the world, and it was good, but Adam and Eve gave in to Satan's lies and disobeyed God. Sin, sickness, and death came into the world. You move farther from God when you sin, and the payment for that sin is death.

But God loved you so much that he gave his son, Jesus, to die on a cross as payment for your sins.

If you tell Jesus your sins, ask for his forgiveness, and ask him to be in charge of your life, he will forgive you. You get to be best friends with Jesus forever on earth and in heaven.
He will always be with you no matter what.

**Here's a simple prayer you can say. Jesus will
hear you just like he heard me.**

*Dear God, thank you for loving me so much that you sent your
son, Jesus, to die on the cross for my sins. Please forgive me for
the wrong things I have done, and wash my heart clean inside. I
want to be best friends with you forever. Show me how to listen
and follow you every day. Thank you for never leaving me.
I love you! Amen.*

This is great news! Now, tell everyone you know.

About the Author

Lauren Breaux is twenty-eight years old and lives at home in North Fond du Lac, Wisconsin, with her mom, dad, and thirty-four-year-old brother Tony (also on the autism spectrum). Lauren can usually be found with her iPad nearby, playing with her cat Kiddo, or on a swing outside. She has a wonderful sense of humor and loves to laugh and make others laugh. Despite her many autistic and cognitive challenges, she is a determined, sensitive, and loving girl.

According to Lauren, "God made me different in a good way."